Even the Mountains

Five Years in a Japanese Village

Sean O'Connor

Alba Publishing

Published by Alba Publishing
P O Box 266, Uxbridge
UB9 5NX, United Kingdom
www.albapublishing.com

A catalogue record for this book is available from the British Library

ISBN: 978-1-910185-60-5

Edited, designed and typeset by Kim Richardson
Cover image: © Junko Oda
Printed by Essentra

10 9 8 7 6 5 4 3 2 1

Contents

Author's Preface – *Shall We Dance?*   5

Introduction   6

The Bucket List   9

To Your Bones   11

Stone Pillows   15

Alive   19

Wildlife   23

Night   29

Our House   33

Garden   39

Palm and Plum   43

Grave Concerns   47

Neighbours   53

'Human Haiku'   57

Longing   61

Jizo   65

Dogen Zenji   69

Kibitsu Shrine   73

Fragility   77

Shaking   81

Mountains   85

Farewell   88

Glossary   90

Acknowledgements   91

About the author   92

For Junko Oda

Author's Preface – *Shall We Dance?*

We met dancing tango.

Junko has a passion for dancing and Argentine tango is by far her favourite dance. She has tangoed in Russia and Italy. Tango was very popular in Dublin at the time and we danced four or five nights a week.

Junko is an enthusiast of Irish history and had lived and studied in Ireland on and off for over twenty years.

Although I had never been to Japan I had held a lifelong intrigue for Japanese culture. As a child I ardently trained in Judo and switched to Aikido in adulthood. My practice of Zen had taken me to Switzerland and America. I had read as widely on the culture and spirituality of Japan as Junko had on Ireland. We had a lot to talk about and those conversations, combined with our love of dancing, led to our marriage.

Within a year of our wedding we moved to a rural village in the prefecture of Okayama on Japan's main island of Honshu where we lived for the next five years. The haiku in this book were written during this time.

In *Even the Mountains,* I have arranged the haiku into themes that are preceded by short passages on different aspects of my experiences living in a Japanese village. The hope is that these passages will be informative in themselves and will also act to animate the haiku that follow them – like music and dance.

Introduction

As an admirer of Sean O'Connor's haiku, first encountered in *Pilgrim Foxes,* I was pleased to be invited to provide this introduction. Doubly pleased, in fact, given that I am something of a Japanophile. A love, beginning with the practice of Soto Zen Buddhism and haiku, deepened and complicated by a short visit to Japan in 2005.

Even the Mountains is an account, in haiku and prose, of Sean O'Connor's five years living in a traditional farmhouse with his wife, Junko, in the rural village of Yuzuri, Okayama Prefecture, on the main island of Honshu.

The hundred-plus haiku are arranged in themed sections, each preceded by a short piece of prose. Lucid and engaging, the prose presents insights into Japanese life and customs, and also locates the haiku in a broader context. The themed sections create a matrix that encompasses the personal (the house, the garden, introductions to village and neighbours, local wildlife, including the snake that lived in the laundry room) and the more general (the Japanese attitudes towards silence and loneliness, transiency and natural catastrophes, the festivals of Obon and Higan).

Jack Kerouac said that haiku should be like porridge – plain and nourishing (although a diet of porridge alone would be dull indeed!). Maybe what he had in mind were haiku like those here. Lean without being slight. The images vivid and direct, without adornment or the distractions of showy wordplay. In addition to the qualities of classical haiku – economy of expression, everyday language (albeit some in Japanese), immediacy and presence - some exhibit the quality of 'lightness' which Basho referred to as *karumi* and highly praised towards the end of his life. Often they are slow burners, requiring a little quiet reflection to reveal their depth. For example, please take a few moments to consider the following:

warm spring sun	nothing moves
a pile of daikon	yet the bamboo
wrinkled	creaks

While, of course, a number of Japanese words, such as *karate, kimono, sushi* and, latterly, *tsunami,* have been incorporated into the English language, much of the Japanese will be unfamiliar to non-Japanese readers. However it is not necessary to be steeped in Japanese language and culture. Where it first occurs, usually in the prose, it is defined and when needed its implications explained. For the remaining terms there is a short glossary at the back of the book. In this way the haiku avoid being encumbered by footnotes. Rather than being obscure, the Japanese gives this collection much of its authentic flavour.

Finally, in conclusion, I would like to pull out two favourites among many:

waiting for guests	Fuji
how silently they sit	inside its mouth
three tea bowls	the shadow of our plane

Stuart Quine

[*Pilgrim Foxes,* Ken Jones, James Norton & Sean O'Connor, Pilgrim Press, 2001.]

The Bucket List

On a Thursday morning in December 2008, Junko and I headed out of Okayama City to go to the office of an estate agent in a rural town. We were buying a house.

It was a typical December day in Okayama. The sky was blue and it was a cold dry day. Okayama train station was busy with people going to work. Our train was relatively quiet as it went north out of the city in the opposite direction to the mass of commuters.

It is customary, when buying a house in Japan, to arrive at the estate agents office with a large bag of cash – enough to complete the entire sale. Not comfortable with that idea we arranged to transfer the money from our bank in advance of signing contracts. I can hear the gasps of western lawyers on reading this.

During the walk from the train to the office we passed a bakery selling special sponge cakes covered in strawberries. Christmas cakes. Well, Japanese Christmas cakes.

It took a while to buy the house. A specially licenced laywer came. The vendor sat across from us. There were introductions, bowing, more introductions, more bowing, tea served, credentials shown, contracts painstakingly gone through (assume bowing for every step mentioned), more tea, more introductions (the boss entered) and, of course, more bowing. It was all over by lunchtime.

And in that little town there weren't many options for lunch. Japanese curry, sushi or KFC.

As we passed the KFC we noticed a large sign in the window explaining that they could not serve any customers for the rest of the day unless they had pre-ordered their 'KFC Christmas Bucket'. That was as close to Christmas as we were going to get. Oh! Did I mention that it was Christmas Day? Well, it was just another day in Japan. No special relevance. But hey! We bought a house.

Christmas Day
the bank staff
in Santa hats

this gift of Christmas cake
a strawberry sponge
– grateful nonetheless

To Your Bones

Our house in Japan had no central heating. We had no insulation either. Most air conditioners can be switched to provide warm air instead of cool for winter time. However, the only room in which we had an air conditioner was the recording studio I had in the attic, and that was to preserve the sensitive electronic equipment from the ravages of the summertime humidity. Like many truly traditional homes in Japan, ours relied on paraffin stoves for heat.

Furthermore, not to be outdone in the retro lifestyle department, we used a traditional *hibachi* for a little heat and to keep a kettle on the boil. This was basically a box with a copper tray with some ash in it, on which we placed red-hot burning charcoal. This leads to a typical experience of feeling warmth on your front and cold on your back. We wore traditional house jackets, called *hanten,* to help us cope.

It is customary to have a very hot bath every evening. You have a shower first, then soak in the piping hot water before getting out and then soaping your body and rinsing off with ladles of water. The purpose of the bath is more relaxation and, in winter, to warm up, rather than merely washing yourself. You warm up to the extent that you could walk naked in snow afterwards.

Winter in Okayama features clear blue skies by day and star-filled, silent nights. It is generally cloudless and there is very little rainfall.

Winter is cold and summer is hot, the Japanese often say. They live this. Even the schools in our locality were only partially heated.

A Canadian, who came during winter to practice Zen in a temple near us, was astonished when sitting *zazen* one freezing morning, to hear the teacher exclaim: 'Feel the cold to your bones.'

steaming
after a bath
snow in the back yard

still dark
through freezing air
our neighbours' cockerels

cold morning
the bamboo grove
groaning

touching our window
disappearing
snow

snow in the garden
the glow of our stove
through *shoji*

this willow's slow sway
swirling through it
    hailstones

Stone Pillows

The Japanese summer is tropical and consists of at least three months of persistant heat and humidity. Here are three numbers that give a sense of the difficulties the summer season generates: twenty metres, forty thousand people and the number two hundred.

When humidity is high on a hot day, leave an air conditioned room and walk only twenty metres outside and you will be drenched in sweat, say, by the time you get to your car. People wear small towels around their necks when outside in order to continuously wipe themselves free of perspiration.

Every summer about forty thousand people in Japan attend hospital emergency rooms for the treatment of life-threatening heatstroke. It kills two hundred people annually.

The heat and humidity is relentless and debilitating, with no reprieve at night. And, as we slept without air conditioning, we did so with windows open and under mosquito nets. On our futon we put a special mat of wooden beads and on our pillows a similar device made with small stones to allow air circulate under our bodies to cool us. It was surprisingly comfortable.

A day is put aside in late spring to prepare. All winter clothes are packed away in see-through vacuum-sealed containers to prevent them from rotting in the oncoming humidity. Expensive electronics, such as good cameras, are stored in de-humidifing cabinets, not unlike small fridges. In autumn this will all be reversed to get ready for winter.

You know it's coming. The five million vending machines in Japan give an indication. Almost overnight they change their stock from mainly hot drinks to cold ones. Shops look different when you enter as they too will have altered to summer goods.

But then, it is also the season of wonderful festivals.

And fireworks!

warm spring sun
a pile of *daikon*
 wrinkled

wild *fukinotou*
soon we will pack away
our winter clothes

awake
my hair wet
on a stone pillow

opening the *shoji*
into coolness
  warmth

with the lantern's sway
from the nearby woodstore
warm waft of resin

my sweat
where it hits the soil
tiny craters

Alive

Consider the hazards one faces when up a ladder during the Japanese summer, engaged in the pruning of persimmon trees. There is the risk of severe dehydration and heatstroke. Snakes are everywhere. Big ones. In trees as well as on the ground below. Then insects. Biting, buzzing, whirling, milling, gnawing, creeping, flying insects.

Touch a centipede and you are poisoned. Not deadly, but you will be in dire pain for a few hours. Tip the hairs of a particular caterpillar and you will be adorned with a mildly painful rash. A sting from a Japanese hornet will cause necrosis of your flesh and a trip to hospital. As to the hornets, they left us alone despite that fact that they had a nest above our back door, and we must have bothered them a bit with our comings and goings.

All of the above can happen, but you are sure of two things: being eaten alive by mosquitoes; and being serenaded (or deafened) by the noise of insects.

Yes, they sure generate plenty of volume when they assemble in chorus, those multitudes of insects. A single cicada can lift you out of it with a piercing call. Get a group of cicadas together and you have one very loud summer choir. And the different types of cicadas have different songs. The favourite for most people (myself included) is the *higurashi*, meaning 'the end of day' cicada as it sings at dusk. It joins the chorus late in summer, signalling (with crickets) the imminent arrival of autumn and its coolness. For that reason too, it is often specified (as are other well known cicadas) in Japanese haiku. In English a cicada is a cicada. The Japanese know them by name, so to speak. The same goes for the different types of crickets and other vocal creatures.

It is not an accident that haiku poets such as Kobayashi Issa wrote hundreds of haiku on insects, from fleas to the praying mantis. Summertime is insect time.

this relentless heat
will it surrender
to this cricket?

I still see them
that warm night
those fireflies

mountain thunder
  silencing
a thousand cicadas

late butterfly
slightly moving
one wing

busy platform
between passing trains
the sound of crickets

sculptor's workshop
long after his death
ants mill about

Wildlife

A snake lived in our utility room. It would occasionally make its way into our laundry basket and startle us. I would simply carry the basket into our side garden and the relieved creature would slip out into the grass. It was a skinny snake with pale green, red, and black bands along its body which made it look like the elongated flag of a forgotten country. Sometimes it would entangle itself around our complicated kitchen tap and I would open the window above the sink to let it free.

However, the decidedly poisonous Mamushi snake was most unwelcome. If one was discovered we would try to kill it with a long-handled shovel.

Frogs, on the other hand, were always welcome. There were ones so tiny that they could sit on your fingernail. Others so slender as to imply poverty. Large, rotund frogs that had a certain stateliness about them. They created quite a racket when they all croaked together in the rice fields around us.

At night, wild boar sneaked out of the bamboo forest behind our house and ate our vegetables. We didn't mind. We were repaid with gifts of wild boar meat from our neighbours who trapped them and butchered them in their yards.

Occasionally we would hear screeching after dark as our cats would square up to a racoon dog.

Fortunately, we were not pestered by packs of wild monkeys. Our carpenter, who lived on the other side of our mountain, was plagued by them. Nor did we encounter any wild bears. There were frequent media reports of wild bears entering towns when food becomes scarce in their mountain habitats.

Our cats had no shortage of prey to hunt. They killed snakes, moles, mice and birds. It all died down when winter came. So much wildlife went into hibernation. With all of the singing insects gone too, winter was remarkably quiet.

this snake and I
the only movement
its tongue

a kingfisher
turning in its hover
its blue blue back

who will bolt first?
  this frog
  this snake

all night
among the forest snakes
the potter's kiln is blazing

old roof beams
the swallows nest
  still empty

finding a dead snake
on its back
my boot print

this old village
even the chickens
   silent

racoon dogs fighting
it reaches the stars
their screeching

this quiet night
wild boar we have never seen
can you hear them?

full laundry basket
my shirt is too big for him
Mister Snake

Night

In Ireland we are accustomed to long winter nights and short ones during summer. However, in Okayama, nightfall occurs by seven-thirty in the evening throughout the year. Dawn is between five and seven in the morning. I found this rather strange for the first year or two.

As with many rural areas, our nights in rural Japan were free of light polution, making for a vivid experience of darkness, stars, and galaxies.

With about two hundred and fifty days of sunshine every year, Okayama is one of the sunniest areas of Japan. Those cloudless skys by day transferred to clear, night skys. This is especially so on winter nights.

Hana-mi, which means flower watching, is the well-known daytime practice of admiring the short-lived blossoming of cherry trees in April, and when done at night is called *yozakura kenbutsu.* There is another practice, lesser known outside Japan, of *tsuki-mi* – enjoying a full moon. Moonlight in rural Japan is a glorious experience. When full, the light is bright enough to cast well defined shadows. Even the shadow of a single pine needle has an eerie clarity. Winter full moon nights are augmented with silence, and if it snows, the hush is deeper still. No need for television, just add *sake.*

By contrast, summer nights are full of the many sounds of insects or, at times, frogs. It can be difficult to sleep on those sultry nights. Lying awake on our stone pillows, with beaded mats on our futons, we would listen to the music of grasshoppers and crickets. It is another kind of silence. The silence of being absorbed in nothing but the here and now.

I once drove to a pond where the countryside meets the outskirts of Kyoto city. I went there to a *tsuki-mi,* to watch the full moon in the presence of friends who are haiku poets. It was a twelve hour return journey by car. With or without *sake,* it was well worth the trip.

a mild night at last
  stars
I have never seen

tonight's moon unseen
a house lamp glowing deeper
in the pond's last light

late evening blue
how alone
this star

dead of night
startled
by my own splash

moonlight shadow
every pine needle
 vivid

early pink blossoms
tonight's full moon
its hint of pink

Our House

Our house in the village of Yuzuri, in the prefecture of Okayama, was a traditional farmhouse called a *kominka*. It was pretty much as you would see in the movies. The flooring was predominantly *tatami* mats or wood. There were no hallways but an *engawa,* or skirting corridor, stretched along the front and one side of the building and had single pane glass from floor to ceiling the length of it. A third wall to the rear of the house was also glass.

This allowed a lot of light in. However, the entirely overhanging roof prevented the burning summer sun from shining directly inside. All along the side of the *engawa* were sliding panels called *shoji*. These are made of light wood and white paper which also allowed light to fill the interior. As the house was surrounded by gardens there was a blurring of a distinction between inside and outside.

On the periphery were rooms with a particular purpose: kitchen, utility room, bathroom, toilet and a lounge known as a 'western room'. That's where the western concept of a room stops. The main area of the house consisted of six connected areas with *tatami* flooring, each with either *shoji* or sliding panels covered in decorated cardboard called *fusuma.*

These panels can be removed or replaced in an instant, allowing for different spaces to be created at a moments notice. By opening or removing the *fusuma* panels you could use the entire area for a large gathering. In winter we would close them all and use just two areas for sleeping, eating, office work and watching TV. That's a big saving on heat!

The Japanese futons we slept on are fold-away matresses without a base. They are stored away during the day so that you can sleep in a different area of the house every night if you wish. Today's dining room can be tonight's bedroom.

moving cloud
the soft glow of *shoji*
slowly brightens

sick in my futon
somehow comforting
the ceiling's wood grain

a world away
the patter of Irish cats
on *tatami* mats

waiting for guests
how silently they sit
three tea bowls

spring
hanging on coat hooks
our *hanten*

lacquer bowls
cleaning them
how they whisper!

in the *tokonoma*
my grandmothers' clock
  silent

moonlit *shoji*
its thin parallel tears
our sleeping cats

pitch dark
my bare feet
on cold wood

the *engawa* lamp
its glow declines
with the rising sun

Garden

Our house had four gardens. To the front, facing south, was a large traditional Japanese garden. Among its trees and rockeries was an imposing, but semi-hidden, stone lantern. Shaded rocks were moss-covered. There were half-buried boulders to step out of the house onto. This garden was built a hundred years ago. What an effort its founders made to place these huge stones in the days of working by hand!

It had three sculpted pine trees that required specialist pruning. Once a year two of our neighbours took care of them. The azaleas, the maple, the plum tree – all needed regular attention. And in summer I hand-sprayed a fine mist of water over the moss to keep it fresh.

The side garden featured hydrangeas surrounded by moss. It was closed in by outbuildings, which included a shed for a single cow (long gone).

Our outbuildings surrounded two sides of the house and most of them were double storey. Behind them all was what we called the 'back garden'. There were two unmarked graves there.

At the centre of the house and buildings was the smallest garden, known in Japanese as a *tsuboniwa*. This literally refers to a space the size of two tatami mats. In standard size that is just under four square metres. Ours was somewhat bigger than that, but our *tsuboniwa* did serve its purpose. It completed a situation in which there was a view of at least one garden from any location inside the house. The blurring of interior and exterior.

We also had a half acre of agricultural land which included a persimmon orchard. We grew all of our vegetables using natural farming methods and exchanged some of our crop with neighbours for peaches and other fruit. We did not need to buy fruit or vegetables for the five years we were there.

in the *tsuboniwa*
deepening the hush
falling snow

nothing moves
yet the bamboo
creaks

this old stone lantern
amplifying
darkness

spring sun after rain
our moss garden
now we see it!

on this green leaf
a tiny dome of water
  its solidity!

in our back garden
fresh flowers
at the gravestones

Palm and Plum

Two trees. Palm and plum.

When we moved into our house there was an enormous palm tree in the side garden. One of our neighbours, a builder, advised that it be removed as it was too tall and would seriously damage the house if it came down in a typhoon. He organised everything: a huge crane, and a team of tree surgeons. For our part, we supplied *sake* and salt – for the ceremony.

As a tree has spirit, it is necessary to sprinkle salt and *sake* while praying for its forgiveness, both before and after cutting it down. So we did.

Our plum tree was in no such danger. To the right of the main door as you came through the gate, it was striking when in blossom. We were leaving winter behind and standing at the edge of spring once the plum blossoms opened. The flowers on our tree were the purest, most vivid, white I have ever seen. A gift of beauty.

And there were other gifts it bestowed. This single tree produced an amazing amount of plums. They were not the large, dark, juicy plums for sale in supermarkets in Ireland. They looked and felt like dark green olives, but twice their size. In plum terms, they were the equivelant of cooking apples and we put them to good use.

Every year one of three large jars of plum wine would mature in our utility room. We would put a new jar into the three year cycle once we broke it open.

In winter we would enjoy pickled plum as a condiment. In summer we used plums in two ways: as a syrup diluted with water it was a refreshing way to stave off dehydration; and we would eat *umeboshi*. These are plums that have been pickled in salt and then dried. An acquired taste, but one worth acquiring as you need to replace salt lost from the body in the heat.

white plum tree
its blossoms
touching stars

on this entire plum tree
just one bud
closed

falling plum blossom
 so slow
its tumble

the plum tree's buds
at last they crack
such whiteness!

stepping out after rain
the scent
of plum

March winds –
hold on plum blossoms
till my wife returns!

Grave Concerns

Whenever my wife and I visited her parents in Kamakura we would hear the *ping!* of a small bell as we put away our coats and settled in. Once greetings were exchanged her father would open an ornate cabinet, called a *Butsudan*, and announce our arrival to the family's ancestors. As ancestors, the Japanese include recently deceased relatives: parents, grandparents, aunties and uncles. The *Butsudan* contains plaques that each represent a person and is inscribed with their details, including the date of their passing. These plaques are usually black and look like minature headstones.

He would light incense, sound the little bowl-like bell, and utter some prayers. In such a manner, the ancestors are invited to special occasions, especially at New Year and the four day festival of Obon during August. Food such as fruit, and drinks such as *sake*, are often placed at the *Butsudan*.

Obon is a four day festival in which the spirits of the dead come to visit. For most of the country this is from the thirteenth to the sixteenth of August, (although some areas celebrate it in July, based on an old calender). In the days leading up to, and after, the August Obon period, you can expect traffic chaos around the major cities of Japan as millions of people travel to and from their hometowns for Obon.

Fires and lanterns are lit outside millions of homes to guide the spirits on Obon's opening day. This is followed by music and dancing in the streets for three days. The dancing (*Bon Odori*) differs from area to area but is always graceful and consists of a series of steps that are easy enough to learn on the spot, making it possible for everyone to join in. On its final night, some areas again light fires and lanterns to see the spirits off. Others go to nearby rivers for *Torou Nagashi*.

Families put a paper lantern with a lit candle inside it onto the waters of a local river and let it float away. In this way, the practice of *Torou Nagashi* allows the spirits of the dead to go back, or float off, to the spirit world.

If a family has suffered any bereavements since the last Obon then they will have a separate lantern for each of their recent losses. In this way, we can clearly see the extent of grief that each family is undergoing. *Torou Nagashi* is a moving experience in which we can appreciate shared grief and fond memories of the departed.

Twice a year, at the times of equinox, in March and September, people go to their family graves to clean and decorate them and to chant for the dead. These periods and their obligations are known as Higan.

Twice a year, during Higan, there would be a sudden increase in passers-by at our house as there were many graves near it. We would see many family groups and individuals walking by with flowers and special pails of water and ladles for cleaning graves. Now and then we would hear their chanting.

The two graves in the garden behind our house had stories about them. It was believed they were the graves of unhappy spirits. One story was that they are the resting place of two servants who had been badly treated by a cruel local landlord who was their master.

It was also said that many years ago a woman in the village suffered a series of unexplained illnesses. She was advised that her sickness may be due to disgruntled spirits in the village whose grave, or graves, were not attended to. The woman cleaned and placed flowers on those two graves and was cured. It is said that from that time, a duty of caring for those graves befell the village. When we bought our house we signed a right of way to those graves to accommodate this.

Occasionally, we would see fresh flowers at those headstones. These were placed there by our next door neighbour.

Higan
living and dead
the graveyard full

water and flowers
on her way to a grave
she bows

headstones
all vertical
except one

the charnel room
deep in its blackness
    gold leaf

all our money gone
winter light gleaming
on these roadside graves

beyond the crematorium
house to house
the postman

distant hill
chants for the dead
  unseen

sowing clover
staring from the bamboo
two gravestones

Neighbours

There was a process. We could not just show up at our newly purchased house with a removals truck and start unloading furniture. We needed to be introduced to the village.

That process began with the estate agent identifying the leader of the village, The *kuchou-san,* and arranging to meet him. She (the estate agent) also needed to figure out how many gifts we should bring for neighbours – and the hierarchy of those gifts. A typical present for such situations consists of a food item for which your hometown is famous. In our case, this meant a particular biscuit from Kamakura. These are dove-shaped and called *Hato Sabure.* We ordered several different sized boxes of these, all gift-wrapped, to be couriered 500 kilometers from Junko's hometown.

After a very pleasant meeting, our new *kuchou-san* introduced us to our nearest neighbour who, in turn, introduced us to her closest neighbours. The biscuits were disappearing. Our introduction to the rest of the village came on the next community work day. On a Sunday morning at 8am, the village gathered for one of its quarterly communal work days. The *kuchou-san* stepped forward and formally welcomed us into the community. Then to work.

It was easy to meet neighbours. They were always working outside, farming, tending their large vegetable gardens, caring for fruit trees and maintaining the irrigation system.

The changing seasons were marked by festivals and gatherings. We had picnics and drank *sake* under cherry blossom trees in April. We ate and danced at the village Matsuri, the summer festival, in the grounds of the school. On New Year's morning we assembled at the shrine.

And of course there were funerals, and births.

There would often be an anonymous box of fruit or vegetables at our door when we returned home.

on our doorstep
left by an unknown neighbour
these bright persimmons

from our carpenter
a gift of rice *nuka*
in a nail box

the news made softer
this gift of pickled *daikon*
her ashes flown home

March sunshine
already they tell stories
about snakes

Smiling

When we moved into the village we were introduced to her – a ninety year old, smiling and gracious lady, who lived with her family close to our new home. She was delighted to meet me, possibily the first foreigner she had met. She beamed as she attempted to pronouce my exotic name and warmly welcomed us into the community.

I would see her as she wandered about chatting with neighbours. We were asked to keep an eye on her. The narrow road in front of our house was used only for access to vegetable plots futher up the hill and had no other dwellings on it. We were oblidged to re-direct her back into the village if she went up there.

To encounter her was always refreshing.

> her dementia
> every day she meets me
> for the first time

There came a time, a couple of years later, when I had not seen her around for a while. We were told she was unwell, that she had pneumonia.

It was not long before a neighbour approached me as I worked outside.

> news she has died
> every stalk in this rice field
> bowing its head

'Human Haiku'

On public transport in Japan mobile phones are switched to silent mode, and if a phone vibrates with an incoming call they are not answered. In the first place, it is illegal to talk on a phone when travelling by bus or train. Law or no law, speaking loudly on public transport is considered impolite and inconsiderate. It can disturb the peace of mind of fellow travellers.

When I first visited Japan I met with the Irish Jesuit priest and writer, William (Bill) Johnson. It was on my first full day in Japan and I recall his parting words as I left Sophia University where he lived. He said that travelling by train in Japan is like being in a moving temple. He was right.

Bill cherished silence. He spent more than half a century in Japan and loved it. Sadly, he took ill and my last visit with him was by his hospital bed. We spoke a little, then, in a manner that is so comfortable for most people in Japan, we spent time in silence together. Days later, he died.

As silence is so valued by the Japanese and, for them, expressions of anger are taboo, it is easy to form an impression of them as aloof and somewhat unemotional. Yet I have rarely encountered such a depth of feeling in people as I did in Japan.

Outwardly, the Japanese appear to be highly conformist. To a large extent this is the case. Their conformity, however, is connected to their strong sense of community, their sense of morality, and the primacy of their consideration of others above individual concerns. Nonetheless, I experienced as much individuality among people there as I have elsewhere.

The following two sections of haiku are in a form known as *senryu*. They are haiku that concern people. The eighteenth century poet who popularised this form is Karai Senryu, whom it is named after. They are sometimes refered to as 'human haiku'.

a tremor
rushing onto the street
    four Lolitas

working all day
and the cat
still sleeping

glad of this soft pencil
writing haiku
on toilet paper

in the supermarket
a monk buying melons
his bald head

travelling monks
delighted to meet
my foreignness

the train full
packed
with silence

Longing

Far from being taboo in Japanese culture, loneliness is openly acknowledged. There is a fondness for bitter-sweet nostalgia. Sorrow and joy often intertwine. The joy in experiencing the beauty of cherry blossoms is tinged with sorrow on realising how short-lived those blossoms are.

Everything is impermanent. Beauty is transient. Our memories may be sweet, but they reside in a past that is gone.

What I am touching on here is the wide range of the emotional repertoire of the Japanese. There are emotional connotations in some expressions in the Japanese language, such as *wabi-sabi,* that are extremely difficult to translate.

We Irish have a long history of mass emigration. Homesickness is a feature of that. For most Irish people there is little positive in that experience. For us, homesickness is a form of sadness. We do not sit comfortably with longing and loneliness. As the haiku that follow give expression to homesickness I experienced when living in Japan, they are likely to be seen by my fellow Irish people as sorrowful.

Most Japanese people will see things differently. They feel the sorrow. But they will sprinkle it with some joy. For them, happiness and sadness are often companions.

However, both the Irish and the Japanese may find some humour here too.

My hankering for Irish tea for example. There I am, living in Japan, and I have the feeling that my life will be incomplete if I don't have Irish tea to drink every day.

When travelling around Japan, especially by train, it is common to see neatly cultivated tea plantations. Indeed, the consumption of tea itself, in the uniquely stylised Japanese Tea Ceremony, has become a world renowned expression of Japanese culture. Yet, in my longing for the comfort of that which is familiar, I spent a fortune importing boxes of Barry's Tea into Japan. Via New York.

midday
I long to ring home
where it is 3am

Tokyo book store
noticing
a friend's name

how familiar!
a letter from Ireland
this handwriting

spring breeze
Irish wind chimes
still unwrapped

a box of Barry's Tea
nothing left
but dust

dense Japanese mist
I long to hear
Dublin's fog horns

Jizo

There are statues everywhere in Japan. Most of these are related to Buddhism. They range in size from just centimeters in height to statues on the scale of the Great Daibutsu in Kamakura which is a thirteen metre tall bronze Buddha that you can walk around inside.

The town of Ofuna is a short distance from the Great Daibutsu. It is a busy, modernised town with rows of bright neon clad fast food joints and pachinko parlours close to its busy train station. Pachinko parlors are Japan's equivalent of gambling halls of the one arm bandits and slot machines type. Overlooking them, on a nearby hill, is a huge statue of Kannon. There is a bench inside it and on the day I entered there was a lady sitting and praying in its tranquil interior.

As you would expect, every temple has statues depicting Buddha. They vary considerably in form and may be found made of stone, wood, bronze or other materials.

But there is one form of statue that is ubiquitous as you travel around Japan – the *Jizo*.

They can be encountered anywhere people have used as a route of travel: on streets, sidestreets, down laneways, by roadsides or along footpaths in remote areas.

Jizo are usually about thirty to sixty centimeters in height. Visitors to Japan often describe them as looking like baby Buddhas. This notion is reinforced by the fact that *Jizo* are frequently adorned with babies' bibs or hats. They sometimes have babies' toys placed beside them.

These statues are depictions of Enlightened Ones who have chosen to help ease our suffering. They are believed to protect those on a journey, whether physical and spiritual. And they protect women and children. The adornments and toys about them have often been put there by women seeking protection for their children, or to assist a deceased child to be happy in the spirit world.

the *Jizo*'s bib
darker
with spring rain

The Great Daibutsu
with this camera angle
almost falling

winter dusk
nineteen stone Buddhas
deepen the silence

statues everywhere
only this *Jizo*
with fresh flowers

deep in the mountain
this *Jizo*'s bib
who cleans it?

glaring pachinko
watching from the hill
all-knowing Kannon

Dogen Zenji

Before departing on my first visit to Japan, Junko asked if there was anywhere I especially wished to see. Eihei-ji, I answered without hesitation. It was an awkward choice as Eihei-ji, a thirteenth century Zen temple founded by Dogen Zenji, lies well off the beaten track in the mountains near the city of Fukui. Our journey to the remote temple from Junko's hometown of Kamakura involved a bus, four trains, a taxi and a short walk in each direction leaving us three hours to spend in the presence of the monks.

If one person can be singled out as having fired my imagination and inspired me to go to Japan it is Dogen.

Back in the 1970s I discovered a handful of books at the gable end, so to speak, of a free-standing book display on the floor of Eason's bookshop in Dublin. Zen books. Writings of Zen masters, books of *koans* and Zen stories. Among them, poems, sayings, and writings by Dogen Zenji.

This was in the days before Zen was commandeered by marketing departments worldwide for the purpose of brand creation. Stick the word 'Zen' in your product title and you imply tranquility, relaxation or peace of mind.

Certainly, the practice of Zen appears tranquil, relaxed and peaceful. And it can be like that. However, Zen practice is as difficult as life itself, and as wonderful. Indeed, I have found nothing to be more challenging.

In 1223 Dogen set out on a dangerous journey to China where he spent four years studying Chan Buddhism. Later, back in Japan, he founded Soto Zen and his temple, Eihei-ji. There are many temples throughout Japan that are architecturally more impressive, no doubt, but it is here that we walk the same ground, hear the same sounds of water gushing in the same rocky stream and smell the same scents as a great poet and spiritual writer, Dogen.

I have yet to return.

the last train to Eihei-ji
distant mountains
   on fire

behind a monk
the swish of his robe
turning petals

night *zazen*
till the moonlight
leaves the room

by my ear
a rush of air
the *kyosaku* strikes

Eihei-ji chanting
noticing my heart beat
with the *mokugyo*

by Dogen's stream
from beyond the universe
birds singing

Kibitsu Shrine

The shaman sits before a cauldron and makes her predictions based on how she interprets the sounds of the water as it boils. This takes place in her high ceilinged, darkened room in a discreet building at the edge of the grounds of the ancient Kibitsu Shrine, about forty minutes' drive from our village in Okayama.

There are, in fact, several shrines in the complex. The main shrine is enormous and sits atop high ground. Its roof is thatched and is designated a national treasure of Japan. Behind it, a four hundred metre, open air, roofed 'corridor' runs down a slope to the far end of the grounds.

Kibitsu Shrine is one of more than 80,000 Shinto shrines throughout Japan, some of which are not much bigger than a telephone box. Each shrine houses one or more gods.

Gods, or spirits, are refered to as *kami* and they are manifold. Mountains, trees, rivers, rocks or some deceased people may be *kami*. The Japanese say there are eight million gods. Some are benefactors, others are to be feared. All are to be respected. Indeed, the ritual we followed when having a tree cut down is an everyday expression of Shinto.

It is said that in Japan one is born in Shinto, lives as a Taoist and dies a Buddhist.

So it is that the Christian Santa comes to children across Japan and many homes put up a Christmas tree and enjoy a Japanese version of Christmas dinner. Then, on New Year's Eve we would go to a local Buddhist temple and queue to ring the temple bell. It is tolled 108 times. Next morning we go the nearby Shinto shrine to gather with our neighbours in a ritual New Year celebration.

Before I recorded the album, *By The Firelight,* I brought the sound engineer, Shin Takai, to Kibitsu to attend a small shrine there for musicians.

Gassho, bow, cast coins, *gassho,* bow.

somehow forlorn
these *kyudo* targets
neatly stacked

my guitar at home
at the musicians' shrine
I cast a coin

waterwheel
  still
    dripping

hidden lantern
the dip of its stone
with age

escaping the broom
a pebble
 bouncing

a door hinge squeaks
and the shaman
wanders off

Fragility

Life is fragile. In a matter of sixty seconds our world can turn upside down. We can die.

One such minute was 2.46pm on March 11th 2011. An earthquake warning sounded through our TV which we left on in the background in case of such alerts. This was a big one. The TV journalists were wearing hard hats in studio and as they spoke the lighting gantry above them began to shake. They could instantly tell us that a very high magnitude earthquake had just occurred off the coast of Tohoku. A tsunami was on its way. We were used to such announcements, or so we thought. No-one expected that this quake was one of the largest for a thousand years.

We watched it all unfold. Houses ripped from their foundations, crashing into each other as they bobbed like corks in the tsunami's torrent. That night we saw live footage of the Tokyo skyline lit up by fires as a nearby oil refinery exploded and burned. It was like war.

Such was the level of trauma that it took some time before we began to realise the significance of the reported damage to the Fukushima nuclear power plant. A human-made disaster triggered by a natural one.

Tsunami and earthquakes are not the only natural disasters faced in Japan. The month of September brings the typhoon season and June, the rainy season. Some typhoons consist only of torrential rain. Rainfall is described in metres, not millimeters. Houses, and even villages, can be swept away in floods along with roads and bridges. Or all of the above may be destroyed by landslides. Sadly, a lady just a few miles from us was killed when a landslide buried her house.

We kept our passports in an emergency bag. It contained enough for us to survive a few days without help should we have to flee. Before bed, we restocked it with fresh water and we slept with our day clothes beside us at the ready.

in case of tsunami
a safe line marked
well above our heads

the typhoon over
on the river's surface
tree tops

our hope for survival
  fresh batteries
  tinned fish

first estimates
ten thousand people dead
since yesterday

fear of radiation
at the fishmonger's
nothing sold

before bed
for the emergency bag
fresh water

Shaking

Before we moved to Japan Junko fancied the idea of living in Tohoku. We checked it out and discovered that it had a high earthquake risk. The area with the lowest risk of quakes was Okayama so we turned our attention to it and subsequently located there.

Having grown up in Kamakura, near Tokyo, Junko had experienced hundreds of earthquakes, but during our first two years in Okayama we hardly noticed them at all. Throughout the six thousand plus islands of Japan there were about 1,500 earthquakes per year, most of them of low level or even imperceptible. Since the great earthquake of March 2011 that has escalated, as has the size of quakes. These days, there are earthquakes somewhere in the country on most days of the week.

There were several occasions when I would be writing at my desk when suddenly my computer would start rocking about, the lightbulb swinging about above me and the walls and partitions shaking noisily as if a huge truck was passing just inches away. Grab the emergency bag and shoes (no time to put them on) and get out of the house quickly.

Seconds later a message will beep on my phone warning me that there is an earthquake. That's the dilemma with earthquake warnings, if you are close, or on, the epicentre then you don't have the few seconds it takes for the warnings to arrive. However, those same warnings can save your life if you are further out from the epicentre in a big quake.

In general we were spared severe or frequent earthquakes down in Okayama. However, in Kamakura, my in-laws (Junko's family name is Oda, meaning: Little Rice Field) had days during which there were numerous quakes that required rapid escapes from their house. These are scary experiences and, because they live close to the sea, there is the ever present fear of tsunami.

conversation stopper
on the other end of the phone
a level six

a minor earthquake
we look at each other
the cat and I

fifteen floors up
my hotel room
    swaying

in the dead of night
a minor quake
through the futon

the classroom trembles
for a passing quake
the lesson paused

earthquakes all day
can we finish it?
this evening meal

Mountains

Mountains in Japan may appear overnight.

Between December 1943 and September 1945, a local postmaster in rural Hokkaido took notes of intense earthquake and volcanic activity in his area. He recorded 200 quakes in one day alone during this time. It turned out that he happened to record the formation of a new mountain which has been named *Showa-shinzan* – Showa New Mountain.

A few months after we moved to Japan there was a large earthquake in a remote part of northern Honshu. Only nine people lost their lives as the area was lightly populated. A TV crew flew over the area in a helicopter and filmed a mountain which had literally been cut in half by the event.

Most of Japan is comprised of mountains and hills and most of these are covered with wild forests. In total, mountains and forests make up nearly 80% of the country.

Only the remaining 20% of Japan is used by humans for agriculture and, by contrast, high density living – big cities.

Fly into Japan via the northern air route from Europe, over Siberia, and you may enjoy a wonderful view of its mountain ranges. Towering above them all, Mount Fuji.

At three times the height of any other mountain in Japan this great volcano maintains a cap of snow all year round. It is common for Fuji to appear to be floating above the clouds, especially during the heat haze of summer. Viewed from any position, it is truly awesome.

Fuji is also formidable, and dangerous. Whilst tens of thousands successfully climb it every year there are regular casualties. In one incident during our time in Japan two professional climbers lost their lives attempting to scale it.

As a teenager I was intrigued by a Zen saying that seemed to me to capture the Japanese sensitivity to the temporary nature of everything. I had not realised how literal the saying could be: *Even the mountains disappear.*

this morning's earthquake
a whole mountain
cut in half

the mountain slides
an elderly neighbour
buried

mountain mist
moving to reveal
one golden tree

through mountain snow
filling the valley
a temple bell

Farewell

For five years we enjoyed life among our neighbours until the day came for us to depart. It was not easy.

Our parting was marked by a gathering of the village in the local hall. Everyone was there. That included dignitaries from other villages such as elected councillors and the headmaster of the nearest school. Well-prepared speeches were read after which people spoke from the floor. In all my life I never experienced such a depth of respect and sincerity. It was difficult to hold back the tears.

To end, they presented us with a formal certificate of their appreciation.

I cannot thank them enough.

Fuji
inside its mouth
the shadow of our plane

Glossary

Daikon – a Japanese winter radish which looks like a large white parsnip but is noteworthy for its smooth surface.

Fukinotou – a wild plant, picked and eaten in February.

Gassho – Japanese for 'palms of the hands placed together', a gesture made as a greeting, in gratitude, or to make a request.

Kannon – a gender neutral Buddhist *bodhisattva* – a person who can reach nirvana but delays in order to help others in their suffering.

Koan – a paradoxical question given by a Zen master (*roshi*) to a student of Zen on which the student meditates and then provides an answer.

Kyosaku – a wooden stick used by Zen teachers to strike students on the shoulders to assist their meditation.

Kyudo – Japanese archery.

Lolita – a female who is part of a fashion subculture in Japan (also called *Lolita*) who wear clothing influenced by Victorian and Edwardian era, or French Rococo, dress.

Mokugyo – a wooden fish-shaped gong used in Buddhism to beat a rhythm during chanting.

Nuka – rice bran. This is used in Japan to pickle vegetables in. In our village we also put rice *nuka* on the land as a fertilizer.

Tatami – rush covered straw flooring panels that are typically 90 cms by 180 cms and about 3cms thick.

Tokonoma – an alcove or recess typically raised a few cms above the floor and used to display flowers and ornaments. The wall of the *tokonoma* is usually adorned with a picture or painting on a long scroll.

Zazen – the practice of sitting meditation in Zen

Acknowledgements

I am deeply indebted to the people of Yuzuri who accepted myself and Junko into the life of their village with kindness, generosity and warmth. Thank you to Oguchi Yuki-san, Osaka Chieko-san, Fukushima-san, Osaka Akira-san, Nanba Shigeaki-san, Tokisue-san, Nanba Masao-san, Adachi-san, Osaka Fumihiko-san and all of their families and our other neighbours in Yuzuri and its surrounding villages. Thanks too to Akaiwa-Shi councilor Kanadani-san, to Kimura-san and to Suei-san for their support and friendship.

My years in Japan were greatly enhanced by my many musician friends there. Thank you Tim Keeler, Scott Chadwick, Shin Takai, Akada-san, Ikeda-san and all my friends in the Bluegrass scene, and the many other wonderful musicians I had the pleasure to perform with. My fondest regards to Nakagawa Kazuko-san and Mayumi-san of Penny Lane in Kurashiki, Kobayashi-san of The Craic Irish Pub in Takamatsu, and to photographer Yukiwo.

Kim Richardson of Alba publishing brought this book to life. I appreciate his friendship and support. Thank you Amanda Bell, James Norton and Kevin Fletcher who read every word of this book and gave valuable feedback. To Stuart Quine for his introduction and for their reviews: Gabriel Rosenstock, Stephen Henry Gill and James Norton. Thank you Denis Grey from Nenagh, Tipperary, and to The Nenagh Writers Group for their encouragement.

Thanks also to the editors of *Meltdown* (Hailstone Haiku Circle, 2013) and the Haiku Ireland anthology, *Stone After Stone* (The Fishing Cat Press, Dublin, 2017) who published some of the haiku in this book.

Special thanks to Junko Oda and her family.

The cover photograph was taken inside our house in Yuzuri by Junko Oda.

About the author

Sean O'Connor is a poet, writer and musician, who currently lives in his native Ireland. *Pilgrim Foxes* (Pilgrim Press, Wales, 2001), co-written with Ken Jones and James Norton, was his first collection of haiku and haiku prose (*haibun*). His second collection, *Let Silence Speak*, was published in 2016 by Alba Publishing.

Sean's haiku have been translated into several languages and published worldwide. During the late 1990s he was an editor of *Haiku Spirit* and, prior to that, co-edited that journal with its founder James Norton. He has toured extensively as a singer and musician, especially in Japan where he performed for five years and recorded the album *By The Firelight*. He currently specialises in performing folk music.

An Honours graduate in Psychiatric Nursing, Sean also holds an M.Phil with Distinction in International Peace Studies from Trinity College Dublin, and has studied psychotherapy and post-graduate management and journalism.

A long time practitioner of Soto Zen, Sean currently lives in rural Tipperary with his Japanese wife, Junko Oda, and their cat, Tono.

You may contact Sean at: mail@seanmusic.com

Other titles by Sean O'Connor

Let Silence Speak, Alba Publishing, 2016.
Pilgrim Foxes, Pilgrim Press, Wales, 2001